RAND NATIONAL DEFENSE RESEARCH INSTITUTE

TRICARE Applied Behavior Analysis (ABA) Benefit

Comparison with Medicaid and Commercial Benefits

Margaret A. Maglione, Srikanth Kadiyala, Amii M. Kress,
Jaime L. Hastings, Claire E. O'Hanlon

Prepared for the Office of the Undersecretary of Defense

Approved for public release; distribution unlimited

For more information on this publication, visit www.rand.org/t/RR1334

Library of Congress Cataloging-in-Publication Data
is available for this publication.

ISBN: 978-0-8330-9286-1

Published by the RAND Corporation, Santa Monica, Calif.

© Copyright 2016 RAND Corporation

RAND® is a registered trademark.

Support RAND
Make a tax-deductible charitable contribution at
www.rand.org/giving/contribute

www.rand.org

Preface

Applied Behavior Analysis (ABA) is a behavioral intervention that aims to improve the functional, communication, and social skills of children with autism spectrum disorder (ASD). The RAND National Defense Research Institute evaluated TRICARE's ABA benefit at the request of the Office of the Under Secretary of Defense for Personnel and Readiness (OUSD [P&R]). The primary purpose of this study was to compare TRICARE's current ABA benefit, including reimbursement rates (defined as third-party payment to the service provider), copayments, and annual caps, with ABA benefits offered by Medicaid and commercial health plans. This study documents the development of TRICARE's ABA benefit; identifies ABA benefits provided by commercial, federal, and state health plans; evaluates market reimbursement rates; calculates a weighted national mean reimbursement rate for several ABA–related services; and assesses the availability of ABA providers in locations with TRICARE beneficiaries who have ASD.

This report will be of interest to policymakers in the U.S. Department of Defense, leaders in commercial and public health care industries, ABA provider organizations, and families of TRICARE beneficiaries who have ASD.

This research was sponsored by the (OUSD [P&R]) and conducted within the Forces and Resources Policy Center of the RAND National Defense Research Institute, a federally funded research and development center sponsored by the Office of the Secretary of Defense, the Joint Staff, the Unified Combatant Commands, the U.S. Navy, the U.S. Marine Corps, the defense agencies, and the Defense Intelligence Community.

For more information on the RAND Forces and Resources Policy Center, see http://www.rand.org/nsrd/ndri/centers/frp.html or contact the director (contact information is provided on the web page).

Contents

Figures

Figures

Tables

Summary

Applied Behavioral Analysis (ABA) is an intervention based on learning theory principles aimed at improving the functional, communication, and social skills of children diagnosed with autism spectrum disorder (ASD). The Office of the Under Secretary of Defense for Personnel and Readiness (OUSD [P&R]) asked the RAND National Defense Research Institute (NDRI) to compare TRICARE's ABA benefit, provided through a new Comprehensive Autism Care Demonstration (ACD), with ABA benefits from other publicly funded programs and commercial insurance plans. OUSD [P&R] was particularly interested in how the proposed TRICARE reimbursement rate of $68 per hour for ABA services performed by a Board Certified Behavior Analyst (BCBA) compares with reimbursement rates in Medicaid and commercial health insurance plans.

This study compared TRICARE's ACD, including reimbursement rates, patient copayments, and annual caps, with ABA benefits offered by Medicaid and commercial health plans. This report provides data on ABA benefits, reimbursement rates in the public and commercial U.S. health insurance markets, and availability of ABA providers by location.

Our initial review of the existing policy and academic literatures did not identify any sources that comprehensively contained this information. We undertook two strategies to ascertain the majority of this information.

In late 2014, the majority of state Medicaid programs that provided ABA services did so through waivers. We identified state Medicaid programs that covered ABA using a comprehensive database on existing state Medicaid Section 1915(c) Home and Community-Based Services waiver-covered services (found at Medicaid.gov) and searches of state websites that reported covering ASD via the waiver system. After identifying state Medicaid programs that covered ABA via the waiver system, we searched state Medicaid fee schedules for ABA provider reimbursement rates. We note here that this search strategy misses information on any state ABA reimbursement rates in the Medicaid programs that covered ABA via their main (nonwaiver) Medicaid program.

We identified a large data source (Truven Health MarketScan® Research Databases) that contains figures on commercial insurance payments for a wide variety of services. Although not a random sample, the MarketScan data in 2013 contained comprehensive outpatient service utilization information on approximately one in four children enrolled in the U.S. commercial health insurance system. We are not aware of any larger existing data source for identifying provider reimbursement rates for ABA services in the commercial insurance market.

In addition to identifying reimbursement rates in the Medicaid and commercial insurance markets in the above manner, we also searched through the Medicaid waiver databases, the academic and policy literatures for information on cost-sharing for ABA services in the private and public health insurance systems. Information on out-of-pocket spending in the private health insurance markets was also derived from analyses of MarketScan data.

ABA Benefit

We did not identify any cost-sharing requirements within the Medicaid waivers filed by states to cover ABA. In the commercial health insurance data that we evaluated, there was a standard (fixed percentage or fixed copay depending on the type of health insurance plan) cost-share for ABA services. We calculated the mean patient out-of-pocket amount for each U.S. state. Mean out-of-pocket spending, as a percentage of the total (insurer and patient) payment, for treatment provided by master's- or doctoral-level providers, known as BCBAs, with the Current Procedural Terminology (CPT) code of H2012 for invoicing, varied across states from 0.4 percent in Michigan to 14.0 percent in Utah. Mean out-of-pocket spending, as a percentage of the total (insurer and patient) payment for therapeutic behavioral health services provided by a bachelor's-level Board Certified Assistant Behavior Analyst (BCaBA), Behavior Technician, or unspecified education-level provider (CPT code H2019), ranged from about 1 percent in Kansas to 12 percent in Ohio.

ABA Reimbursement Rates

We found substantial state variation in provider reimbursement rates for ABA services within the Medicaid and commercial health insurance systems. Herein, the reported commercial insurance rates represent third-party payment to the service provider and do not include patient cost-share amounts.

In fall 2014, state Medicaid reimbursement rates for a BCaBA or behavior technician ranged from $25 to $75 per hour. For providers with a master's degree (required for BCBA certification) or doctorate (required for certification as a BCBA-D), Medicaid reimbursement rates varied from $55.50 to $125 per hour. According to 2013 commercial health insurance claims data, mean state reimbursement rates in the commercial insurance sector varied from $24.64 to $160 per hour for a provider with a bachelor's degree or an unspecified education level (BCaBA or Behavioral Technician). For providers with a master's degree or doctorate, reimbursement rates in the commercial health insurance system varied from $36.90 to $196.50 per hour.

The mean national reimbursement rate, derived from this commercial data and Medicaid information, weighting the state-level results by the number of children diagnosed with ASD in each state, was $65.16 per hour for therapeutic behavioral services (H2019) from a BCaBA, Behavioral Technician or unspecified-level provider, or $94.72 per hour for master's- or doctoral-level providers. Sensitivity analyses using information on state-level utilization rates resulted in weighted average calculations that were very similar. In sum, the $68-per-hour reimbursement rate proposed by TRICARE for services provided by a BCBA (which requires a master's degree) is more than 25 percent below the U.S. mean.

The state variation in Medicaid and commercial reimbursement rates identified in this report implies that a single U.S. rate for TRICARE as a whole may not be sustainable in areas where the TRICARE rate is substantially below the prevailing local rate. For example, if TRICARE adopted the $68-per-hour rate for one-to-one ABA provided by a BCBA or BCBA-D proposed in September 2014, the TRICARE rate would be below the mean commercial insurance rate in the first ten states where data were available and above the mean commercial insurance rate in the other seven states. Providers in those ten states might be disincentivized to accept TRICARE patients compared with enrollees from other private health insurance plans.

ABA Provider Locations

To identify locations of potential ABA provider shortages, we obtained data from the Behavior Analyst Certification Board (BACB) on the location of all board certified ABA providers in the United States as of May 2015, and then calculated the number of children (younger than 18) with ASD in TRICARE per each provider in larger ZIP code–based geographic areas throughout the United States.

Fifteen areas with potential TRICARE ABA users (children with ASD) had no board certified ABA providers. The number of children with ASD in TRICARE in those ZIP code–based locations ranged from 12 in southern Missouri to 288 in western Idaho. Locations with a high number of potential TRICARE ABA users per certified provider include several sites in the Southwest (San Diego, southern Arizona, and west Texas) and in the Southeast (Virginia, South Carolina, Georgia, and Alabama). These locations have more than 100 potential TRICARE users for each BCBA.

There are currently no best practice standards as to the number of board certified providers per number of children with ASD. According to 2012 BACB guidelines, the average caseload for a BCBA supervising focused treatment without support from a BCaBA is ten to 15 children; with a supporting BCaBA, the average caseload is 16 to 24 children (BACB, 2012). As our analysis included only potential users in TRICARE, we were unable to calculate potential overall caseloads; this would require estimates of the entire number of children with ASD in each ZIP code location. Unfortunately, such data are not available.

Conclusions

Coverage and reimbursement rates for ABA vary widely in both commercial plans and Medicaid programs throughout the United States. We were asked to compare TRICARE's proposed rate of $68 per hour for one-to-one ABA therapy provided by a BCBA or BCBA-D, reduced from $125 per hour, with the current U.S. market. The proposed $68-per-hour rate is below the mean commercial insurance rate in ten of the 17 states where data figures were available and above the mean commercial insurance rate in the other seven states. Compared with 14 states that specify rates for master's- and doctoral-level ABA providers in Medicaid, the $68-per-hour rate is below the reimbursement rate in 11 states. Based on local Medicaid and commercial insurance reimbursement rates, weighted by the number of children with ASD covered by each type of insurance in each location, the weighted mean U.S. reimbursement rate for ABA services performed by a BCBA or BCBA-D is $94.72.

Acknowledgments

We would like to acknowledge exceptional administrative support from Katherine Mariska and excellent advice from Sue Hosek, who provided quality assurance and important feedback throughout the project. We thank Ross Anthony and Barbara Wynn, who provided critical feedback on this report. All are with the RAND Corporation. Kristie Gore and John Winkler of the RAND National Defense Research Institute provided study guidance and oversight. We thank Casey Hunter of RAND for performing analysis of ZIP code data on location of board certified ABA service providers and potential ABA users enrolled in TRICARE. We thank Cathy Zebron of RAND for technical assistance in report preparation. Truven Health Analytics, Santa Barbara, California, skillfully performed analysis of deidentified MarketScan data from commercial health insurance companies. Defense Health Agency leadership, including TRICARE Regional Office staff and Managed Care Support Contractors, provided important input. Finally, we thank Dr. Laura Junor, former Principal Deputy Undersecretary of Defense for Personnel and Readiness, for initiating this project.

CHAPTER ONE

Introduction

Background

Autism Spectrum Disorder

Autism spectrum disorder (ASD) and autism are general terms for a range of complex disorders of early brain development. ASD diagnoses combine several conditions (autistic disorder, pervasive developmental disorder or not otherwise specified [PDD-NOS], and Asperger syndrome), which were diagnosed separately until the fifth edition of the Diagnostic and Statistical Manual of Mental Disorders was implemented in 2013 (American Psychiatric Association, 2013). These disorders manifest in a wide range of limitations in social interaction and communication (verbal and nonverbal). The U.S. Centers for Disease Control and Prevention (CDC) estimates that 1 in 68 children in the United States has an ASD (CDC, 2015). In fiscal year (FY) 2010, there were approximately 23,500 TRICARE beneficiaries (about 1 percent) diagnosed with ASD out of the 2.2 million military dependents age 18 and younger (Zickafoose et al., 2013).

At present, no cure exists for ASD. The current approach is to provide early intervention treatment services to help modify and improve behavior and social skills, along with treating and preventing childhood illnesses. These early intervention treatment services have been shown to improve a child's development (Maglione et al., 2012).

Applied Behavior Analysis

Applied Behavior Analysis (ABA) is an approach to early intervention treatment designed and supervised by qualified professionals. ABA is the systematic application of a range of interventions based on learning theory principles. ABA has been shown to increase good or useful behaviors (e.g., functional, communication, and social skills) through reinforcement procedures and reduce negative behaviors (e.g., self-injury) (Maglione et al., 2012). ABA may be used to develop basic skills (e.g., looking, listening) in addition to more-complex skills (e.g., reading, communicating). The optimal level of ABA necessary to achieve measurable benefits has not been established; however, functional improvement has been observed with 20 or more hours per week, and most studies using 30–40 hours of ABA per week observed positive results (Maglione et al., 2012). To date, many treatments, including ABA, have been characterized as nonmedical (Office of the Secretary of Defense, 2010), which has implications for health insurance benefits.

Board Certified Behavior Analysts (BCBAs, also referred to as Behavior Analysts) develop and oversee the delivery of ABA. The certification of master's-level (BCBA) and doctoral-level (BCBA-D) providers is relatively new, beginning with the creation of the Behavior Analyst Certification Board (BACB) in 1998 (BACB, 2015). One-to-one ABA therapy can also be provided by Board Certified Assistant Behavior Analysts (BCaBAs, also referred to as Assistant Behavior Analysts) and Behavior Technicians supervised by a BCBA or BCBA-D, but initial patient assessment and treatment planning must be performed by a BCBA or BCBA-D. Assistant Behavior Analysts are trained to supervise Behavior Technicians; however, TRICARE requires that supervision be performed by a BCBA or BCBA-D.

Problem Statement

Until July 2014, TRICARE covered ABA through a combination of programs. As of July 25, 2014, the TRICARE Comprehensive Autism Care Demonstration (ACD), also commonly referred to as the Autism Care Demo, combined all ABA services into one demonstration project and expanded coverage for ABA to all beneficiaries with ASD. The ACD is scheduled to end on December 31, 2018 (Defense Health Agency [DHA], 2015a). TRICARE generally bases its reimbursement system on Medicare, which primarily serves older adults, and the ABA benefit, which is directed toward children, has not been directly compared with the ABA benefits offered by other health plans or through government programs. Thus, the Office of the Under Secretary of Defense for Personnel and Readiness (OUSD [P&R]) asked the RAND National Defense Research Institute (NDRI) to describe TRICARE's ABA benefit and compare it with other publicly funded programs and commercial insurance plans. OUSD [P&R] was particularly interested in how the proposed TRICARE reimbursement rate of $68 per hour for ABA services performed by a BCBA compares with reimbursement rates (defined as third-party payment to the service provider) in Medicaid and commercial health insurance plans.

Project Overview

We examined the TRICARE ABA benefit, including its evolution over time, and compared it with ABA benefits provided by Medicaid and commercial health insurance plans. Our comparison included an analysis of provider reimbursement rates, patient copays, and annual limits across a range of ABA providers (e.g., Behavioral Analysts, Assistant Behavior Analysts, and Behavior Technicians). Upon completion of the reimbursement rate analyses, at the request of the sponsor, we estimated the weighted mean reimbursement rates for each state (where data permitted) and the United States as a whole. Lastly, we identified locations of potential provider shortages based on the number of TRICARE beneficiaries with ASD and the number of board certified ABA providers. All information may be used by the sponsor in making modifications to the TRICARE ABA benefit structure.

Outline of the Report

The remainder of the report is divided into three main sections. In the next chapter, we compare ABA coverage in TRICARE with ABA coverage in Medicaid and commercial insurance. We begin with a description of the ABA benefit in TRICARE historically and then progress to coverage of ABA in the ACD. We then proceed to a description of

ABA coverage in the public (Medicaid) and commercial health insurance systems. Then, we identify and calculate reimbursement rates for ABA among public (Medicaid) and private payers, describe some results from an informal survey of providers regarding their willingness to accept key price points and using the available state-level data to calculate national weighted means for ABA provider reimbursement. In Chapter Four, we provide some data on provider availability for ABA treatment across the United States. Chapter Five contains a Discussion section.

CHAPTER TWO

Coverage of ABA–Comparison of TRICARE with Medicaid and Commercial Insurance

TRICARE ABA Benefit

In this section, we summarize TRICARE's ABA benefit, particularly the services currently covered by TRICARE and how covered services have evolved from the Extended Care Health Option (ECHO) in 2005 to the ACD in 2014. To summarize the TRICARE ABA benefit, we reviewed publicly available information via Federal Register (FR) notifications; Code of Federal Regulations (CFR); state and national court cases, decisions, and appeals; and the National Defense Authorization Acts (NDAA), with a focus on those that include discussion of ABA (Public Law 107-107, 2015; Public Law 109-364, 2006; Public Law 112-479, 2012). We also reviewed the information presented for beneficiaries and providers on the DHA and Managed Care Support Contractor (MCSC) websites, including TRICARE Operations and Policy Manuals. Finally, given the rapid evolution of the TRICARE's ABA benefit during this evaluation, we held a meeting with key DHA officials and reviewed DHA-provided documentation that was not yet publicly available. We also coordinated with OUSD [P&R] and other relevant agencies/offices to compile all information necessary to summarize the TRICARE ABA benefit.

We reviewed the following components of TRICARE's ABA benefit:

- covered services
- eligibility criteria for the ABA benefit, including age limits and specific diagnosis of autism

- costs to beneficiaries for ABA services, including copays by TRICARE plan (Prime, Standard/Extra), beneficiary category (active duty, retirees, Guard/Reserve or active-duty family member [ADFM], non-active-duty family member [NADFM]), and service location (in network, out of network), annual out-of-pocket limits, maximum annual amount covered by TRICARE, and relationship to beneficiaries' catastrophic cap
- permissible ABA providers, provider requirements, and in-network versus out-of-network providers
- other key benefit characteristics (e.g., initial testing requirements, prior authorization requirements, authorization renewal frequency).

History of the TRICARE ABA Benefit

Program for Persons with Disabilities (PFPWD)

TRICARE first offered ABA coverage in 2001 under its PFPWD, which provided financial assistance to qualifying beneficiaries who were "moderately or severely mentally retarded or seriously physically disabled" (Office of the Secretary of Defense, 2004). Although the PFPWD provided financial assistance to reduce the disabling effects of a qualifying condition, it was not intended to be a stand-alone benefit. Under the PFPWD, TRICARE authorized ABA as a cost-shared educational benefit.

Extended Care Health Option

Section 701 of the NDAA for FY 2002 required the Department of Defense (DoD) to establish a military health program providing extended benefits to eligible dependents to "assist in the reduction of the disabling effects of a qualifying condition of an eligible dependent" (Public Law 107-107, 2015). To comply with this mandate, DoD established the TRICARE ECHO, which replaced PFPWD and went into effect on September 1, 2005. Under ECHO, qualifying ADFM beneficiaries may receive benefits beyond what was available through the TRICARE Basic program (DoD, 2004). ABA was a subset of Intensive Behavioral Intervention (IBI) services, behavioral interventions considered special education services, which were provided through ECHO because they were not covered under TRICARE Basic (DoD, 2007).[1] Participation in the ECHO program required enrollment in the applicable military service's Exceptional Family Member Program (EFMP) (DoD, 2004). To be eligible for the ECHO program, a beneficiary had to have "moderate or severe mental retardation," "a serious physical disability," or "an extraordinary physical or psychological condition," as defined in Section 199.2 of Title 32 of the U.S. Code of Federal Regulations (DoD, 2004).

Enhanced Access to Autism Services Demonstration (ECHO Autism Demo)

In an effort to expand services for children with ASD further within the existing ECHO program, Section 717 of the NDAA for FY 2007 required DoD to develop a plan to provide services to military dependents with ASD (Public Law 109-364, 2006). To accomplish this mandate, DoD implemented the Enhanced Access to Autism Services Demonstration (hereinafter, ECHO Autism Demo) in March 2008 and expanded IBI services, including ABA, to eligible ADFM beneficiaries in the TRICARE ECHO program (DoD, 2007). The purpose of the ECHO Autism Demo was to permit DoD to determine whether its provider model increased access and provided services to the most appropriate population, and whether quality of service standards and state requirements for IBI (including ABA) providers were being met (DoD, 2010).[2] The ECHO Autism Demo initially was to remain in

---

[1] The TRICARE Basic program is the legal term used for the primary medical benefits authorized under chapter 55 of title 10 of the U.S. Code and 32 C.F.R. § 199.4. (32 C.F.R. §199.2) It includes plans such as TRICARE Prime, TRICARE Standard, TRICARE Extra, TRICARE Reserve Select, TRICARE Retired Reserve, and TRICARE for Life. (TRICARE Policy Manual, 2008).

[2] In its announcement of the ECHO Autism Demo, DoD described the gaps in its then-current provider model. Under 32 C.F.R. §199.6(e)(2)(ii)(B), an ECHO outpatient care provider included an individual, corporation, foundation, or public entity predominately rendering services of the type allowable as an ECHO benefit. 32 C.F.R. §199.6(f) permitted certain accommodations to be considered a TRICARE-authorized individual professional provider. Prior to the ECHO Autism Demo, TRICARE authorized IBI services only by ABA-trained outpatient care providers who were generally individual practitioners (DoD,

effect for two years, but it was extended in 2010 (DoD, 2010) and 2011 (DoD, 2011), with a final expiration date of 2014.

ABA Pilot

On January 2, 2013, Section 705 of the NDAA for FY 2013 required DoD to create a pilot program to further provide for the treatment of ASD, including through ABA. The purpose of the pilot program was to assess the feasibility and advisability of establishing a beneficiary cost-share for ASD treatments, and to compare treatment provision of the ECHO program with other TRICARE programs. The pilot was authorized for a maximum of one year (July 2013–July 2014), and it provided a supplemental benefit for NADFM beneficiaries with ASD who had limited ABA coverage through TRICARE Basic starting in August 2012.

During this one-year period, TRICARE covered ABA services for different beneficiary populations through either the ECHO Autism Demo (ADFM) or the ABA Pilot (NADFM). These piecemeal, temporary programs were how TRICARE covered ABA until the ACD went into effect in 2014. Figure 2.1 illustrates the development of TRICARE's ABA benefit until the ACD.

Key components of TRICARE's ABA coverage immediately before the ACD (TRICARE Basic, ECHO Autism Demo, ABA Pilot) and during the new ACD are presented in Table 2.1. In both the ECHO Autism Demo and the ABA Pilot, the minimum age for ABA was 18 months and ABA was provided under a tiered delivery model. In this model, BCBAs conduct assessments, develop treatment plans, and supervise the BCaBAs and behavior technicians who implement the treatment plan with the beneficiary. In both of these demonstrations, there was a $36,000 annual TRICARE cap on reimbursement. Cost-sharing varied from the ECHO enrollment fee for active-duty

---

2007). However, DoD noted that its practices often were not incorporated and did not meet the requirements for the 32 C.F.R. § 199.6(f) accommodations to qualify as a corporate service provider (DoD, 2007). The demo was designed in part to expand the pool of eligible "corporate service providers" of ABA services.

Figure 2.1
TRICARE ABA Benefit Timeline

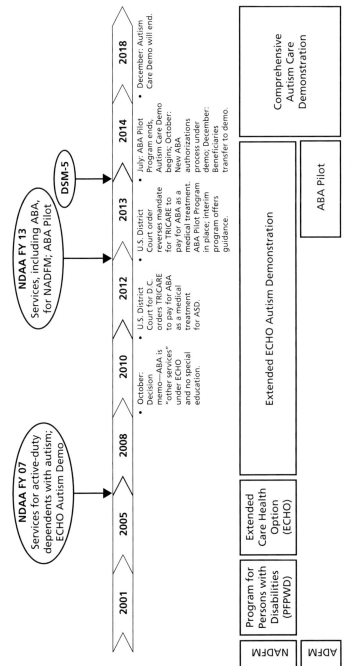

RAND RR1334-2.1

Table 2.1
TRICARE ABA Coverage Immediately Before and During the ACD

	TRICARE Basic	ECHO Autism Demo	ABA Pilot	Comprehensive Autism Care Demonstration
Eligible beneficiaries	All	ADFM	NADFM	All
Diagnosis	Primary care provider or specialized ASD diagnosing provider			
Referral required	No	Yes	Yes	Yes
Age limits	Not specified	18 month minimum	18 month minimum	No minimum or maximum age
ABA delivery model	Sole provider	Tiered delivery	Tiered delivery	Tiered delivery
Clinical appropriateness review	No	No	Yes (two years)	Yes (two years)
Prior authorization	No	Yes (every six months)	Yes (annual)	Yes (annual)
Test requirements	No	Recommended, not required	ADOS-2[a]	Referring physician: Physician-primary care manager (P-PCM)–yes; ADOS-2[a] required ASD provider–no
Progress assessments	No	Yes (every six months)	Yes (every six months with Vineland-II[b])	Yes (every six months)
Treatment plan	Not specified	Required	Required	Required
TRICARE cap on reimbursement	None	$36,000/year	$36,000/year	None

Table 2.1—Continued

	TRICARE Basic	ECHO Autism Demo	ABA Pilot	Comprehensive Autism Care Demonstration
Beneficiary cost	Based on beneficiary category and plan	ECHO enrollment fee	10% cost-share	TRICARE Basic–varies by beneficiary category and TRICARE plan

SOURCE: DHA, 2015a and DoD, 2015

[a] Autism Diagnostic Observation Schedule, Second Edition (ADOS-2) (Lord et al., 2012) is a standardized assessment tool.

[b] Vineland Adaptive Behavior Scales, Second Edition (Vineland-II) (Sparrow, Cicchetti, and Balla, 2005) measures adaptive skills.

service members in the ECHO Autism Demo to 10-percent cost-shares for NADFM in the ABA Pilot.

Comprehensive Autism Care Demonstration

The ACD combines all TRICARE ABA services for all beneficiary categories and TRICARE health plans into one demonstration. The ACD was first announced in the Federal Register in June 2014 (DoD, 2014) and was updated in May 2015 (DoD, 2015). The ACD started on July 25, 2014, aimed to have all covered beneficiaries receiving ABA transitioned to the ACD by December 31, 2014, and will continue through December 31, 2018. In announcing the ACD, DoD acknowledged that as of June 2014, there were not established uniform ABA coverage standards in the U.S. (DoD, 2014). Its own previous ABA benefits were provided through "a patchwork" of "various temporary authorities."[3] In combining all existing temporary ABA policies into a

---

[3] The Federal Register notice (DoD, 2014) announcing the ACD stated:

> Faced with various temporary authorities and the resulting complexity of the current interim TRICARE policies concerning coverage of ABA for ASD, [DoD] will create a new comprehensive Autism Care Demonstration providing all TRICARE-covered ABA under one new demonstration. This will encompass ABA services that recently have been provided under a patchwork of the TRICARE Basic Program (i.e., the medical benefits authorized under Section 199.4 of title 32, Code of Federal Regulations), the ECHO

single program, DoD sought to incorporate lessons learned from previous TRICARE ASD programs and "ensure continued ABA coverage for all TRICARE beneficiaries . . . diagnosed with ASD." (DoD, 2014; DoD, 2015). With the ACD, the DoD also sought to:

- further analyze and evaluate the appropriateness of the ABA tiered-delivery model under TRICARE in light of BACB guidelines
- determine the appropriate provider qualifications for the proper diagnosis of ASD and the provision of ABA
- assess the feasibility and advisability of establishing a beneficiary cost-share for the treatment of ASD
- develop more efficient and appropriate means of increasing access and delivering ABA services under TRICARE while creating a viable economic model and maintaining administrative simplicity (DoD, 2014).

Under the ACD, TRICARE reimburses services for ABA and other related services for beneficiaries with an ASD diagnosis. The services covered under the demonstration include: functional behavioral assessments, initial ABA assessment (functional behavioral assessment) and treatment plan, one-on-one ABA therapy, monitoring progress toward treatment goals, supervision of subordinate ABA providers, and training of caregivers. ABA therapy provided in a group is not covered. There are no duration limits for ABA services and the ACD removed the government's cost-share annual limit ($36,000).

Originally, the ACD had notably different cost-share rules based on beneficiary category and TRICARE plan (Table 2.2). Most importantly, the one-on-one ABA services provided by BCaBAs and registered behavior technicians (RBTs) were included in the ECHO

Autism Demonstration (i.e., the supplemental ABA benefits authorized for certain active duty family members under Section 199.5 of title 32, Code of Federal Regulations), and the ABA Pilot (i.e., the supplemental ABA benefits authorized for certain non-active duty family members—including retiree dependents and others—under Section 705 of the National Defense Authorization Act (NDAA) for Fiscal Year (FY) 2013.

monthly cost-share for ADFM whereas NADFMs had a 10-percent cost-share that did not count toward their annual catastrophic cap.

Given the tiered-delivery model, beneficiaries, especially NADFMs, were concerned about their costs. In a tiered delivery model, BCBAs conduct assessments, develop treatment plans, and supervise the BCaBAs/RBTs who implement the treatment plan with the beneficiary. During the course of this project, a notice (DoD, 2015)

Table 2.2
Autism Care Demonstration—ABA Cost-Share by Beneficiary Category and Plan

Beneficiary category	TRICARE Plan	Original ACD Cost-Share		Final ACD Cost-Share
		BCBA/BCBA-D	BCaBA/RBT[a]	ABA Services
ADFM[b]	Prime	Copay: $0	ECHO monthly cost-share	Copay: $0
	Standard/ Extra	15% in-network; 20% out-of-network	ECHO monthly cost-share	15% in-network; 20% out-of-network
Retiree family member	Prime	Copay: $12	10%	Copay: $12
	Standard/ Extra	20% in-network; 25% out-of-network	10%	20% in-network; 25% out-of-network
Guard/Reserve	TRICARE Reserve Select	15% in-network; 20% out-of-network	10%	15% in-network; 20% out-of-network
	TRICARE Retired Reserve	20% in-network; 25% out-of-network	10%	20% in-network; 25% out-of-network

[a] In original cost-share plan, services provided by BCBA/BCBA-D apply to annual catastrophic cap ($1,000 for active-duty, TRICARE Reserve Select; $3,000 for retirees); services provided by BCaBA/RBT did not apply toward annual catastrophic cap.

[b] ADFM required to register for ECHO to participate in the ACD. ECHO cost-share for every month that ECHO benefits are used are based on service member rank (range: $25 [E1–E5] to $250 [O-10]).

amended the ACD to address these concerns about out-of-pocket costs and in anticipation of the development of guidelines and/or best practices for ABA therapy from the BACB and other experts. Specifically, the cost-shares for all ABA services under the ACD were realigned with the TRICARE Basic program and all cost-shares accrue to the beneficiaries' annual catastrophic cap ($1,000 for active-duty, TRICARE Reserve Select; $3,000 for retirees).

In September 2014, TRICARE announced that reimbursement rates for services provided by Behavior Analysts would be reduced by 46 percent from $125 per hour to $68 per hour (DHA, 2015b). This plan was put on hold and reimbursement rates will be updated as relevant data are available.

Comparison of TRICARE ABA Benefit with Medicaid and Commercial Health Plan ABA Benefits

Next, we compare the TRICARE ABA benefit with information on ABA coverage benefits in the Medicaid and commercial health insurance systems. Thirty-seven states and the District of Columbia have laws related to insurance coverage for ASD and 31 states require coverage of treatments for ASD (National Conference of State Legislatures, 2012).[4] We obtained information on Medicaid and commercial insurance plans to compare ABA coverage, annual cost or quantity limits, reimbursement rates, and patient copays with those of TRICARE's Autism Care Demo.

State Medicaid programs vary dramatically from state to state in terms of eligibility criteria and benefits provided to children eligible for participation in the program. Medicaid coverage of services for ASD is incredibly dynamic; the past few years have seen a host of changes in coverage of ABA due to legislation, litigation, and new evidence on the effectiveness of treatments. State Medicaid programs that pro-

---

[4]   Alabama, Alaska, Arizona, Arkansas, California, Colorado, Connecticut, Florida, Illinois, Indiana, Iowa, Kansas, Kentucky, Louisiana, Maine, Massachusetts, Michigan, Missouri, Montana, Nevada, New Hampshire, New Jersey, New Mexico, New York, Pennsylvania, Rhode Island, South Carolina, Texas, Vermont, Virginia, West Virginia, and Wisconsin.

vide ABA services initially provided them through waiver programs, a mechanism that is widely used by states to provide Medicaid services to children with intellectual or developmental disabilities. In July 2014, the Centers for Medicaid and Medicare Services (CMS) issued clarification on coverage of behavioral services for children with ASD. CMS stated that Medicaid plans must cover ASD treatment services that are deemed medically necessary to ameliorate behavioral conditions (Mann, 2014). CMS does not mandate coverage of ABA; however, ABA is one of the most commonly used behavioral interventional for children with ASD. Thus, some states that had elected to cover services through waivers are in the process of updating the Medicaid state plan in order to ensure that federal financial participation is available for expenditures for these services. During the course of this project, some states (e.g., California, Connecticut) were in the process of moving ASD services out of the waiver plans into general state plans.

We were not aware of any source that contained comprehensive information regarding whether a particular state's Medicaid program covered ABA. Thus, to understand Medicaid coverage of ABA, we focused on Medicaid's waiver system mentioned previously. Waiver data are available from every state that uses this mechanism because states are required to submit detailed plans to the federal government regarding coverage of waiver services (types of services covered, any limitations on quantity of services, any limits on spending per child, etc.).

We approached identification of state Medicaid waiver coverage of ABA in two ways:

1. We searched all waiver applications to identify those that specifically proposed covering children diagnosed with ASD. We then searched each of these identified waivers for explicit mentions of ABA as a covered service.
2. For states that covered children with ASD via the waiver system but did not report coverage of ABA within the waiver, we also undertook a search of that particular state's Medicaid website to determine whether ABA was one of the covered services.

The above procedures determined a pool of 24 states that covered ABA via the state Medicaid waiver system and identified services covered, caps on the amount of hours or expenditures per year, and eligibility requirements.

We gathered information on commercial health insurance coverage of ABA from publicly available health plan manuals and brochures. Consumer materials described services covered by the plans, while materials for providers listed Current Procedural Terminology (CPT) codes for invoicing. These materials rarely listed reimbursement rates; so we analyzed data from Truven Health MarketScan® Research Databases, the largest available commercial health insurance claims database in the United States. In 2013, MarketScan data captured information on approximately 10 million children enrolled in commercial health insurance, a figure that represents approximately 25 percent of the children in the U.S. commercial health insurance market. MarketScan data contain provider reimbursement and copayment data on all reimbursed services, including ABA. We analyzed MarketScan data from 2013, which was the most recent year available when we started our project in fall 2014.

In order to identify claims from children with ASD in MarketScan databases, we first limited data to individuals younger than 18 years of age. After identifying individuals based on age, using the MarketScan outpatient data files, we defined a child as having a diagnosis of ASD if he or she had at least two outpatient claims with at least one of the International Classification of Diseases, Ninth Revision (ICD-9) codes listed in Table 2.3.

Table 2.3
ICD-9 Codes Used to Identify ASD

Code	Diagnosis
299.00 – 299.01	Autistic disorder
299.10 – 299.11	Childhood disintegrative disorder
299.80 – 299.81	Other specified pervasive developmental disorders (Asperger's syndrome)
299.90 – 299.91	Unspecified pervasive developmental disorder

After identifying children diagnosed with ASD using the selection criteria in Table 2.3, we identified all outpatient claims with the Healthcare Common Procedure Coding System (HCPCS) and CPT codes displayed in Table 2.4, per the materials we identified describing instructions for invoicing for ABA services (Anthem Blue Cross Blue Shield, 2015; Priority Health, 2014; Tufts Health Plan, 2014; United Health Care, 2014). The primary CPT codes used by commercial insurance plans to represent ABA provision are H2012 (representing the hourly rate for Behavioral Analyst) and H2019 (representing one-to-one ABA, 15-minute increments, often by an Assistant Behavior Analyst or Behavior Technician). Some commercial plans also use modifier codes to indicate the education level of the provider (e.g., doctoral or master's level), but our explorations of the MarketScan data indicated that only a very small percentage of identified claims included these modifiers. Plans also use codes H0031 and H0032 to represent provision of an initial assessment and development of a treatment plan. We used these data to study patient copayments. These data were also used to estimate mean reimbursement rates and utilization patterns by state. For both the cost-sharing and reimbursement rates analyses, we only use data from states with a minimum of 30 claims. Although we use this minimum cutoff to estimate the relevant statistics, because the data is deidentified and claims are not from a random sample, standard errors on these statistics are likely to be understated.

Medicaid ABA Coverage

We identified documentation for ABA coverage through waivers in Medicaid programs in 24 states. For several states, we identified multiple waivers related to ASD. Waivers at a minimum described the services covered, quantity or cost limits on services, maximum annual willingness by the state to spend on enrollees, and cost-sharing. In a few instances, waivers also contained information on reimbursement rates that states expected to pay providers for ABA services.

The findings are summarized in Table 2.5; states are organized by the three TRICARE regions. For all states in the table, we confirmed that ABA was one of the waiver-covered interventions by review of waivers and searches of state Medicaid websites. Three other states

Table 2.4
CPT Codes Used to Invoice for ABA

Code	ABA Services
H0031	Mental health assessment by nonphysician
H0032	Mental health service plan development by nonphysician
H2012	Behavioral health per hour, usually BCBA or BCBA-D
H2019	Therapeutic behavioral services, per 15 minutes (often provided by BCaBA or Behavior Technician)

(Maine, Mississippi, and New Mexico) report coverage of behavioral services for ASD and use codes that are typically used to cover ABA services; however, because we could not confirm coverage of ABA, they are excluded from the table.

According to waivers accessed in fall 2014, eight states that cover ABA have explicit limits on the quantity of behavioral treatment. Limits range from eight hours per week listed in Connecticut's Early Childhood Autism Waiver to 40 hours per week listed in South Carolina's waiver for Pervasive Developmental Disorder. Only two states have explicit annual dollar limits with respect to ABA: South Carolina limits ABA costs to $50,000 per year, while Utah's annual cost limit is $29,300. However, 11 states have waivers that put annual dollar limits on total spending on ASD services. Annual cost limits range from $16,176 to $135,000. The median annual cost limit is $30,000, while the mean is about $42,000. These limits are in line with TRICARE's previous annual limit of $36,000. The current TRICARE ACD demonstration program has no quantity or cost limit on services.

Importantly, there was no cost-sharing required in any of the identified Medicaid waivers. This was not unexpected, as cost-sharing is generally not required for most Medicaid services to children (Selden et al., 2009).

Table 2.5
Medicaid Benefits by TRICARE Regional Office (TRO) and State

State	Limit on Number of ABA Sessions: None, Not Reported (NR), or Hours	Limit on Behavioral Treatments: None, NR, Amount, or Hours	Dollar Limit on Total Treatment: None, NR, Amount	Program Title	Additional Limits on Amount of Waiver Services (C-4 Section of Waivers)
TRO North					
Connecticut	8.5 hours/week	$30,000	$30,000	Early Childhood Autism Waiver	None
Illinois	None	None	$16,176	Support Waiver for Children and Young Adults with Developmental Disabilities	Individuals allocated budget amounts based on need
Indiana	None	None	None	Community Integration and Habilitation Waiver	Individuals allocated budget amounts based on need
Indiana[a]	None	None	$16,545	Family Supports Waiver	None
Maryland	25 hours/week	25 hours/week	None	Waiver for Children with Autism Spectrum Disorder	None

Table 2.5—Continued

State	Limit on Number of ABA Sessions: None, Not Reported (NR), or Hours	Limit on Behavioral Treatments: None, NR, Amount, or Hours	Dollar Limit on Total Treatment: None, NR, Amount	Program Title	Additional Limits on Amount of Waiver Services (C-4 Section of Waivers)
Massachusetts	None	$25,000	$25,000	Children's Autism Spectrum Disorder Waiver	None
Michigan	None	None	NR	Eligible for Medicaid or MiChild	NR
New Hampshire	None	None	$30,000	NH In Home Supports Waiver for Children with Developmental Disabilities	None
New Jersey	25 hours/week	25 hours/week	None	Renewal Waiver	Allocated budget amount based on need
North Carolina	None	None	$135,000	Comprehensive Waiver (3.5)	None
North Carolina[a]	None	None	$17,500	Comprehensive Waiver (3.5)	None

Table 2.5—Continued

State	Limit on Number of ABA Sessions: None, Not Reported (NR), or Hours	Limit on Behavioral Treatments: None, NR, Amount, or Hours	Dollar Limit on Total Treatment: None, NR, Amount	Program Title	Additional Limits on Amount of Waiver Services (C-4 Section of Waivers)
Virginia	None	None	None	Individual and Family Developmental Disabilities Support Waiver	None
Wisconsin	Early Intensive Behavioral Intervention: 30–40 hours/week—no more than three years of services	None	Cost limit (but NR)	Children's Long Term Support Developmental Disability Waiver	None
TRO South					
Arkansas	30 hours/week	None	None	Autism Waiver	Behavioral treatments limited to three years
Florida	None	None	None	Developmental Disabilities Individual Budgeting Waiver	Individuals allocated budget based on need (risk predictions)
Louisiana	None	None	$16,410	Children's Choice Waiver	None

Table 2.5—Continued

State	Limit on Number of ABA Sessions: None, Not Reported (NR), or Hours	Limit on Behavioral Treatments: None, NR, Amount, or Hours	Dollar Limit on Total Treatment: None, NR, Amount	Program Title	Additional Limits on Amount of Waiver Services (C-4 Section of Waivers)
South Carolina	40 hours/week	None	$50,000	Pervasive Developmental Disorder	None
(TRO West)					
California	None	None	None	Home and Community-Based Services Waiver for Californians with Developmental Disabilities	None
Colorado	None	None	$25,000	Home and Community-Based Services–Children with Autism Waiver	None
Idaho	None	None	None	Children's Developmental Disabilities Waiver	Individuals allocated budget based on evidence based research and need

Table 2.5—Continued

State	Limit on Number of ABA Sessions: None, Not Reported (NR), or Hours	Limit on Behavioral Treatments: None, NR, Amount, or Hours	Dollar Limit on Total Treatment: None, NR, Amount	Program Title	Additional Limits on Amount of Waiver Services (C-4 Section of Waivers)
Idaho[a]	None	None	None	Act Early Waiver	Individuals allocated budget based on evidence based research and need
Kansas	200 units/year for autism specialist; 100 units/week for intensive individual support person	None	None	Autism Waiver	Limited to three year, unless medically necessary
Missouri	180 days plus additional 90 days possible (waiver)	None	$22,000	Autism Waiver	None
Missouri[a]	270 days plus additional 90 days	270 days plus additional 90 days	$12,000	Partnership for Hope	None
Montana	None	None	None	Children's Autism Waiver	Spending caps for ancillary services, not ABA

Table 2.5—Continued

State	Limit on Number of ABA Sessions: None, Not Reported (NR), or Hours	Limit on Behavioral Treatments: None, NR, Amount, or Hours	Dollar Limit on Total Treatment: None, NR, Amount	Program Title	Additional Limits on Amount of Waiver Services (C-4 Section of Waivers)
Nebraska	None	None	$100,000	Autism Waiver	None
North Dakota	None	None	None	Autism Spectrum Disorder Birth through Seven	None
Utah	None	None	None	Community Supports Waiver for Individuals with Intellectual Disabilities & Other Related Conditions	None
Utah[a]	None	None	None	Medicaid Autism Waiver	None

NOTE: Waiver as of November 2014.

[a] States listed twice have more than one waiver.

Commercial Insurance

Because Medicaid waiver programs do not typically require patient copayments for ABA services,[5] we compared TRICARE's ABA copayment levels with those in the commercial insurance market. Table 2.6 presents the share, where available from the MarketScan data, of the total payment (insurer reimbursement and patient cost-share amount) that is due to the patient cost-share for H2012 and H2019 (no modifier) by state. The table also provides the information on the number of claims used to construct each of the statistics. Mean out-of-pocket spending for H2012 ranged from 0.4 percent in Michigan to 14.72 percent in Utah. Mean out-of-pocket spending for H2019 ranged from 0.96 percent in Kansas to 12.17 percent in Ohio. It is important to note that the median out-of-pocket spending was zero for H2012 in 11 states and zero for H2019 in six states. We note here that because the data were deidentified (both patient identifier and insurance plan were redacted), it was not possible to know if a patient had reached his or her out-of-pocket maximum. Thus, it is likely that the calculated out-of-pocket spending statistics are lower-bounds for plan cost-sharing values.

Regarding annual coverage limits for ABA, we are not aware of any source of data on a representative sample of commercial insurance plans and a survey of all commercial insurance companies was beyond the scope of this project.

Summary

Consistent with other services provided to children by Medicaid, we did not find any cost-sharing for ABA in state Medicaid programs. For private insurance, we find average out-of-pocket percentages that are consistent with standard cost-shares ($5/$10 copays or 10-percent to 20-percent cost-shares). TRICARE cost-sharing rates in the ACD are similar to out-of-pocket spending rates found in the MarketScan data.

---

[5] Selden et al. (2009) surveyed cost-sharing in Medicaid and CHIP programs in 50 U.S. states and District of Columbia and found minimal to no cost-sharing for services to children.

Table 2.6
Commercial Insurance, Mean Out-of-Pocket Cost as a Share of Total Payment by TRO and State

	Patient Copayment Percentage, H2012 (N)	Patient Copayment Percentage, H2019 (N)
State (TRO North)		
New Jersey	4.10 (229)	5.58 (2070)
New York	9.11 (315)	not available
North Carolina	11.64 (190)	not available
Ohio	not available	12.17 (247)
Illinois	7.21 (92)	10.57 (779)
Massachusetts	3.85 (996)	3.68 (8339)
Michigan	0.40 (87)	1.69 (5644)
Pennsylvania	not available	9.18 (1473)
Wisconsin	8.64 (150)	6.44 (2649)
State (TRO South)		
Florida	9.48 (638)	8.08 (3103)
Tennessee	not available	2.83 (92)
Texas	12.22 (616)	6.47 (1902)
State (TRO West)		
Arizona	not available	3.33 (1332)
Colorado	not available	10.45 (216)
Iowa	not available	3.63 (113)
Kansas	not available	0.96 (408)
Minnesota	10.38 (1091)	6.70 (616)
Missouri	not available	8.60 (2618)
Nebraska	not available	9.43 (43)
Oregon	4.63 (45)	not available
Utah	14.72 (479)	not available
Washington	4.35 (355)	not available

CHAPTER THREE

Reimbursement Rates for ABA, Medicaid, and Commercial Insurance

In this section, we identify and calculate ABA reimbursement rates in the Medicaid waiver and private health insurance systems. To identify Medicaid reimbursement rates in waiver states that covered ABA, we searched each state's website (as mentioned in Chapter Two) for the most-recent physician/health care provider reimbursement pay schedules. In the majority of cases, we were able to identify a state Medicaid fee schedule from 2014 that included information on ABA reimbursement rates. When identifying reimbursement information, we also looked specifically for any rate differentiation by the education level of the provider. In the majority of fee schedules, ABA reimbursement used CPT code H2019. A few states used CPT codes H2012 and H2014 for reimbursing ABA. It is important to note that in June 2014, the American Medical Association published, for the first time, CPT Category III codes for ABA (American Medical Association, 2014). However, few states had implemented these codes by January 2015, when we completed retrieving reimbursement information on the Medicaid plans.

For commercial insurance plans, using the MarketScan data, we calculated the mean and median reimbursement rate for each state, for each of the HCPCS and CPT codes displayed in Table 2.6 in Chapter Two. These means and medians did not include patient cost-share, which was calculated separately and discussed in Chapter Two. We excluded the top and bottom 1 percent of claims for all of the states because claims data typically include some errors. An examination of the distributions of reimbursement by state indicated that we had to apply stricter criteria for eight additional states. As one might expect, outlier criteria only affected the means and had no effect on the median reimbursement values. As noted previously, for external validity, we only report mean and median reimbursements for codes that have a minimum of 30 claims in a given state. We reiterate that although we use this minimum cutoff to estimate the relevant statistics, because the data is deidentified and claims are not from a random sample, standard errors on these statistics are likely to be understated. Finally, due to data confidentiality, MarketScan databases could only provide information for Connecticut, Maine, New Hampshire, Indiana, South Carolina, Kentucky, Louisiana, Idaho, Montana, and New Mexico in one combined category, referred to as "other." Thus, these states were excluded from our analysis of commercial insurance data.

Prevailing Reimbursement Rates for ABA Services

Medicaid

We searched each state's Medicaid website for the most-recent physician/health care provider reimbursement pay schedules applicable to ABA. In the majority of states, ABA is reimbursed using the H2019 HCPCS code, representing 15 minutes of therapeutic behavioral services. Where noted, some states (e.g., California, Florida, and Massachusetts) use other codes. In some cases, the waiver provided more-detailed information than the Medicaid fee schedules. The data sources and corresponding CPT codes for each state are displayed in Table 3.1. These were the most recent schedules available online as of January 2015.

Table 3.1
Sources for Medicaid Reimbursement Rates by TRO and State

State	CPT Code for Reimbursement Rate	Year
TRO North		
Connecticut	H2019 code found under both Medicaid behavioral health fee schedule and special services fee schedule. Codes from both fee schedules are reimbursed at the same rate	2015
Illinois	H2019—Medicaid mental health services fee schedule	2006
Indiana	H2019—Medicaid fee schedule	2015
Maryland	Figure from waiver, not fee schedule	2015
Massachusetts	T2013—MA Department of Developmental Services fee schedule	2015
New Hampshire	H2019—NH Medicaid fee schedule	2013
New Jersey	H2019—Medicaid fee schedule - TJ (Children's Service) modifier	2015
North Carolina	H2019—Community Alternatives Programs-Intellectual/Developmental Disabilities Waiver fee schedule	2013
Virginia	H2019—Medicaid fee schedule	2015
Wisconsin	H2012—Medicaid fee schedule	2015
TRO South		
Arkansas	H2019—Medicaid autism waiver fee schedule	2015
Florida	T1027—Medicaid fee schedule	2014
Louisiana	90849 (Applied Behavioral Analysis)—From Children's Choice Waiver fee schedule	2015
South Carolina	H2014—Rehabilitative behavioral health services provider fee schedule	2015
TRO West		
California	H2019—Temporary rates vary by county, per MediCal rep	2015
Colorado	H2019—Child autism waiver fee schedule	2015

Table 3.1—Continued

State	CPT Code for Reimbursement Rate	Year
Idaho	H2019—Medicaid children's developmental disability codes	2014
Kansas	H2019 and H2015—From the 2011 Kansas Autism Policy Manual	2012
Missouri	H2019—Other services Medicaid fee schedule	2015
Montana	H2019—Medicaid fee schedule	2015
Nebraska	H2014—Medicaid fee schedule for mental health and substance use services	2015
North Dakota	H2021—Medicaid fee schedule	2015

Table 3.2 displays the reimbursement rates identified by state, organized by TRICARE region. As noted previously, H2019 is invoiced in 15-minute increments; for easy comparability with reimbursement rates for H2012, which is billed in hourly increments, we report rates for the period of one hour. Where we were able to ascertain rates for different provider levels, these rates are displayed in the second and third columns. This information in some instances came from review of waivers,[1] rather than fee schedules. The far right column displays the rates abstracted from the fee schedules listed in Table 3.1.

Rates varied widely across the United States. Coastal states in the Northeast, such as Connecticut, Massachusetts, and New Jersey, reimbursed doctoral-level providers at more than $100 per hour. This is notably more than TRICARE's proposed rate of $68 per hour. In contrast, Florida's Medicaid program recently reduced the hourly rate for BCBA supervisory services to $55.50 per hour and the rate for direct ABA provision to $50 per hour, regardless of provider level. Compared with 14 states that specify rates for master's- and doctoral-level ABA providers in Medicaid, the $68-per-hour rate is below the reimbursement rate in 11 states. Where provider level of education or certification

---

[1]   We note within the table cells when a particular reimbursement rate was taken from waivers instead of fee schedules.

was not specified, rates for one-to-one ABA therapy ranged from $14 to $101 per hour. This wide range may reflect several factors, including level of provider education and experience, practice costs, malpractice insurance costs, local cost of living, state budget priorities, and local provider advocacy.

Table 3.2
Medicaid Reimbursement Rates by TRO and State

State	Reimbursement per Hour, Master's or Doctoral Level [a]	Reimbursement per Hour, Bachelor's Level or Tech [a]	Program Title	Therapeutic Behavioral Services Hourly Rate (H2019 Unless Noted)[a]
TRO North				
Connecticut	$123.60	$75.00	Early Childhood Autism Waiver	$75.00
Illinois	NR	$71.00, behavior intervention and treatment (from waiver)	Support Waiver for Children and Young Adults with Developmental Disabilities	$54.72 to $63.48
Indiana	$90.00 to $105.00 for intensive behavior intervention—Level 1	$70.00	Community Integration and Habilitation Waiver	$90.00 to $105.00, doctorate; $70.00, mid-level
Maryland	NR	$65.80, intensive individual support services (from waiver)	Waiver for Children with Autism Spectrum Disorder	NR
Massachusetts	$125.00, doctorate or highly experienced master's; $100.00, recent master's	$48.00, tech	Children's Autism Spectrum Disorder Waiver	$125.00, doctorate; $100.00, master's (uses T2103)
New Hampshire	NR	NR	NH In Home Supports Waiver for Children with Developmental Disabilities	$93.84

Table 3.2—Continued

State	Reimbursement per Hour, Master's or Doctoral Level [a]	Reimbursement per Hour, Bachelor's Level or Tech [a]	Program Title	Therapeutic Behavioral Services Hourly Rate (H2019 Unless Noted) [a]
New Jersey	$113.00, doctorate; $85.00, master's	$73.00, bachelor's	Renewal Waiver	$113.00, doctorate; $85.00, master's; $73.00, bachelor's
North Carolina	$101.24, behavior consultant—Level 3; $72.92, behavior consultant—Level 2	NR	Comprehensive Waiver (3.5)	$72.92, Level 2; $101.24, Level 3
Virginia	$89.00, urban; $81.00, rural	NR	Individual and Family Developmental Disabilities Support Waiver	$89.00, urban; $81.00, rural
Wisconsin	NR	$35.00, counseling and therapeutic services (from waiver)	Children's Long Term Support DD Waiver	$32.53 (uses H2012)
TRO South				
Arkansas	NR	$72.00	Autism Waiver	$72.00
Florida	$55.50, master's	$50.00	Developmental Disabilities Individual Budgeting Waiver	$50.00 (uses T1027); $56.00 (T1024)
Louisiana	$118.24, BCBA (CPT code 90849)	$78.00, BCaBA	Children's Choice Waiver	$118.00, master's or doctorate; (uses 90849)

Table 3.2—Continued

State	Reimbursement per Hour, Master's or Doctoral Level [a]	Reimbursement per Hour, Bachelor's Level or Tech [a]	Program Title	Therapeutic Behavioral Services Hourly Rate (H2019 Unless Noted) [a]
South Carolina	$67.53, Early Intensive Behavioral Intervention Plan Implementation (from waiver)	$33.76, Lead Therapy; $15.52, Line Therapy II (from waiver)	Pervasive Developmental Disorder	$31.34 (uses H2014)
TRO West				
California	Announced in September 2014 that it would cover ABA; no state rate established as of January 2015	Announced in September 2014 it would cover ABA; still no rate established as January 2015	HCBS Waiver for Californians with Developmental Disabilities	Los Angeles County[b] $52.00, bachelor's; $75.00, master's or doctorate
Colorado	$87.00, behavioral therapy, lead therapist (H0004)	$14.12	HCBS Children with Autism Waiver	$87.00, behavioral therapy, lead therapist (H0004); $14.12, other
Idaho	$64.80	$44.40	Children's Developmental Disabilities Waiver	$64.80, master's; $44.40, bachelor's
Kansas	NR	$25.00, intensive individual support	Autism Waiver	$25.00, bachelor's; $70.00, master's or doctorate (uses H2015)

Table 3.2—Continued

State	Reimbursement per Hour, Master's or Doctoral Level [a]	Reimbursement per Hour, Bachelor's Level or Tech [a]	Program Title	Therapeutic Behavioral Services Hourly Rate (H2019 Unless Noted) [a]
Missouri	$92.73, senior behavior consultant; $77.24, behavioral consultant	NR	Autism Waiver	$92.73, senior behavioral consultant; $77.24, behavioral consultant
Montana	NR	NR	Children's Autism Waiver	$27.04
Nebraska	$87.04, licensed psychologist; $63.57, supervising behavior therapist (from waiver)	$37.41, lead behavior therapist; $26.79, ABA tech (from waiver)	Autism Waiver	$29.00 (uses H2014)
North Dakota	NR	NR	ASD, birth through 7 years old	$75.76 (uses H2021)
Utah	$57.84, behavior consultation III (from waiver); $80, intensive individual support-consultation services (from waiver)	$21.32, behavior consultation I; $37.76, behavior consultation II (from waiver); $28 intensive individual support-direct service (from waiver)	Community Supports Waiver for Individuals with Intellectual Disabilities & Other Related Conditions	$68.08

NOTES: Waivers as of November 2014
[a] Unless noted, all reimbursement rates are from fee schedules accessed January 2015.
[b] California statewide rate yet to be determined.

Commercial Insurance

The following reimbursement figures are presented from analyses of the MarketScan data conducted by Truven Health Analytics. Table 3.3 displays mean hourly third-party reimbursement for H2019, the CPT code most often used by commercial insurance plans to invoice for one-to-one ABA therapy. Mean hourly reimbursement ranged from $24.64 in Ohio to $160.00 in North Carolina. Median rates ranged from $20.80 in Ohio to $105.32 in Arizona.

Although ABA is often performed by Assistant Behavior Analysts and Behavior Technicians under supervision of a BCBA or BCBA-D, the H2019 data makes no distinction as to the provider type or level of education. Most major commercial health plans (including Blue Cross, Blue Shield, Optum/United Healthcare, Tufts, and Aetna) use H2019 to invoice for ABA by a paraprofessional. A few health plans use a modifier to indicate provider level; for example, the CPT code H2019-HO indicates that the provider has a master's degree. Unfortunately, there were far too few claims with modifiers for meaningful analysis.

Table 3.3
Hourly Reimbursement Rates, Therapeutic Behavioral Services (H2019 with no modifier), Commercial Insurance by TRO and State

State	Claims (N)	Insurance Payment	
		Mean	Median
TRO North			
Illinois	779	$42.76	$40.00
Maryland	107	$60.00	$44.00
Massachusetts	8,339	$56.08	$52.00
Michigan	5,644	$48.96	$50.00
New Jersey	2,070	$66.16	$50.00
New York	1,114	$52.80	$52.40
North Carolina	1,503	$160.00	$100.00
Ohio	247	$24.64	$20.80
Pennsylvania	1,473	$52.84	$38.40

Table 3.3—Continued

| State | Claims (N) | Insurance Payment | |
		Mean	Median
Virginia	270	$80.40	$53.20
West Virginia	409	$87.20	$57.20
Wisconsin	2,649	$50.56	$40.00
TRO South			
Florida	3,103	$78.48	$50.28
Georgia	67	$77.60	$50.00
Tennessee	92	$75.00	$75.00
Texas	1,902	$75.60	$56.00
TRO West			
Arizona	1,332	$91.08	$105.32
California	37,193	$53.60	$50.00
Colorado	216	$54.00	$45.00
Kansas	408	$51.08	$50.00
Minnesota	616	$46.52	$43.20
Missouri	2,618	$34.72	$32.52
Nebraska	43	$44.60	$53.32
Nevada	689	$48.04	$45.00
Oregon	2,352	$118.28	$45.00
Utah	928	$62.40	$50.00
Washington	584	$99.20	$50.00

Table 3.4 displays mean hourly third-party reimbursement for H2012, the CPT code used by many commercial plans to invoice for ABA services performed by a BCBA or BCBA-D. Mean hourly reimbursement ranged from $36.90 in Missouri to $196.50 in Georgia. Median rates ranged from $25.00 in Missouri to $180.00 in Georgia. The proposed $68-per-hour rate is below the mean commercial insur-

ance rate in ten of the 17 states where data was available and above the mean commercial insurance rate in the other seven. The unweighted mean and standard deviation for commercial values were $68 and $28.

Table 3.4
Average Hourly Reimbursement Rates, Behavioral Health by Nonphysician (H2012), Commercial Insurance by TRO and State

State	Claims (N)	Insurance Payment	
		Mean	Median
TRO North			
Illinois	92	$67.17	$70.83
Massachusetts	996	$92.86	$96.00
Michigan	87	$74.10	$75.00
New Jersey	229	$122.75	$142.50
New York	315	$72.40	$75.00
North Carolina	190	$61.37	$62.50
Virginia	192	$67.20	$45.40
Wisconsin	150	$46.50	$38.00
TRO South			
Florida	638	$65.14	$66.60
Georgia	101	$196.50	$180.00
Texas	616	$142.04	$120.00
TRO West			
California	1,658	$98.90	$75.00
Minnesota	1,091	$43.96	$38.33
Missouri	497	$36.90	$25.00
Oregon	45	$115.90	$121.50
Utah	479	$79.60	$80.00
Washington	355	$113.70	$103.80

Table 3.5 displays the mean third-party reimbursement for H0031, the CPT code used by many commercial plans to invoice for patient assessment, in preparation for development of an ABA treatment plan. In TRICARE's ACD, this must performed by a BCBA or BCBA-D. In commercial insurance plans, mean reimbursement ranged from $25.62 in Missouri to $192.39 in Maryland. Median rates ranged from $24.00 in Missouri to more than $100 in ten states. The unweighted mean and standard deviations for the commercial values are $88 and $41.

Table 3.5
Average Reimbursement Rates, Mental Health Assessment by Nonphysician (H0031), Commercial Insurance by TRO and State

State	Claims (N)	Insurance Payment	
		Mean	Median
TRO North			
Illinois	107	$110.74	$100.00
Maryland	33	$192.39	$113.92
Massachusetts	2,001	$98.13	$108.33
Michigan	279	$115.19	$121.67
New Jersey	203	$62.49	$31.00
New York	342	$92.90	$90.00
Ohio	65	$111.10	$103.99
Wisconsin	70	$126.00	$120.00
TRO South			
Florida	254	$86.73	$90.00
Georgia	60	$116.21	$96.00
Texas	155	$120.80	$120.00
TRO West			
Arizona	39	$92.54	$90.00
California	2,498	$136.31	$100.00

Table 3.5—Continued

| State | Claims (N) | Insurance Payment | |
		Mean	Median
Missouri	279	$25.62	$24.00
Nevada	38	$123.14	$120.00
Oregon	105	$104.40	$120.00
Utah	72	$104.72	$100.00
Washington	177	$65.46	$38.75

Table 3.6 displays the mean third-party reimbursement for H0032, the CPT code used by many commercial plans to invoice for development of an ABA treatment plan. In TRICARE's ACD, this must performed by a BCBA or BCBA-D. In commercial insurance plans, mean reimbursement ranged from $17.41 in Pennsylvania to $136.18 in Arizona. Median rates ranged from $12.25 in New York to at least $110.00 in four states. Nine out of the 23 states providing data had median reimbursement rates of at least $100.00.

Table 3.6
Average Reimbursement Rates, Mental Health Service Plan Development by Nonphysician (H0032), Commercial Insurance by TRO and State

| State | Claims (N) | Insurance Payment | |
		Mean	Median
TRO North			
Illinois	171	$42.15	$28.33
Massachusetts	66	$73.23	$85.00
Michigan	339	$95.04	$110.00
New Jersey	181	$86.93	$70.00
New York	267	$48.16	$12.25
North Carolina	63	$43.83	$27.08
Pennsylvania	6,554	$17.41	$14.50

Table 3.6—Continued

State	Claims (N)	Insurance Payment	
		Mean	Median
Virginia	46	$101.37	$105.00
Wisconsin	95	$67.10	$60.00
TRO South			
Alabama	33	$31.60	$21.25
Florida	419	$43.70	$20.00
Georgia	74	$111.83	$110.00
Texas	234	$105.33	$108.75
TRO West			
Arizona	98	$136.18	$116.00
California	20,884	$128.67	$110.00
Colorado	43	$85.38	$85.00
Missouri	752	$23.89	$22.00
Nevada	155	$96.86	$100.00
Oregon	213	$126.39	$100.00
Utah	148	$87.74	$90.00
Washington	208	$107.88	$94.50

Willingness of ABA Providers to Accept Key Price Points

In September 2014, TRICARE announced that reimbursement rates for BCBA/BCBA-Ds would be reduced by 46 percent, from $125 per hour to $68 per hour (DHA, 2015b). RAND was tasked with informally assessing whether ABA providers would continue to serve TRICARE clients, given the proposed rate decrease. Due to the short timeline for this project, it was not practical to conduct a survey of providers. Conducting such a survey would require approval by a Human Subjects Protection Committee and the federal Office of Management and Budget, which might take several months or more. Thus, a comprehensive survey of ABA providers was beyond the scope of this project. Our team conducted an informal qualitative assessment of the possible consequences of TRICARE's adoption of these key price/rate points on the willingness and ability of ABA providers to continue to accept TRICARE. To evaluate provider willingness, we met with key DHA and TRICARE officials, representatives of ABA provider agencies, and a representative of the U.S. Marine Corps Exceptional Family Member Program (EFMP).

To abide by the rules set forth by the Paperwork Reduction Act, we spoke with fewer than nine non-federal "key informants," who represented ABA provider agencies throughout the United States. The largest agency provided ABA services in 14 diverse states. In sum, they indicated that providers in large metropolitan areas would not accept the rate decrease, as $68 per hour is well below both public and commercial reimbursement rates in these localities. Some providers expressed the belief that $68 per hour would be acceptable in localities with low practice costs and cost of living where market rates are similar.

We also met with a representative of the U.S. Marine Corps EFMP who told us that several Marines were unable to accept desired assignments due to lack of ABA providers in the assigned locations. Instead, these Marines accepted assignments near locations where providers were available, such as San Diego, California.

We met with staff from the TRICARE Regional Offices (TROs) and their Managed Care Support Contractors (MCSCs), and behavioral health subcontractors in January 2015. The following organizations were represented:

- TRO North: HealthNet and Managed Health Network
- TRO South: Humana and Value Options
- TRO West: United Healthcare, Military & Veterans (M&V), and Optum.

A HealthNet representative reported they had not encountered a beneficiary who was unable to access ABA services due to the lack of a provider. One Value Options representative made a general inquiry of her staff and found that most beneficiaries who were on a wait list chose to be there because they were waiting for a specific individual ABA provider. The other Value Options representative reported having more than enough providers for the number of beneficiaries.

TRO West reported previous waitlists in the Missouri–Kansas border area, Washington state, and El Paso, Texas. In response to the staff shortage, their contractors, United M&V and Optum, reached out to their commercial provider networks to recruit new TRICARE ABA providers. In addition, they reached out to national and local advocacy groups and community based organizations to broadcast the need for additional providers. Using these methods, they doubled the number of providers in the TRICARE ABA network. They acknowledged there are still occasional waits of four to six weeks for the initial assessment because it must be performed by a BCBA or BCBA-D.

Estimate National Mean Reimbursement Rates for ABA

Ideally, a national mean reimbursement rate is a weighted average of local reimbursement rates that combines local geographic information on reimbursement rates in the public and commercial health insurance sectors with information on the quantity of services received in those local markets. Using such data to calculate a mean national reimbursement rate ensures that the final results accurately reflect the variation in rates and service utilization across the country; that is, that rates in highly populated areas and areas of heavy utilization are adequately represented. To implement an approach based on these principles, we first searched for state-level information on the number of children diagnosed with ASD in commercial and public health insurance plans and information on state-level ABA utilization rates.

Information on Children with ASD in Public and Commercial Health Plans

We used the 2012 National Survey of Children's Health (NSCH) to identify state-level information on the number of children diagnosed with ASD in commercial and public health insurance plans. The NSCH is a nationally representative data set aimed at understanding the health status and health care needs of U.S. children. It is fielded approximately every four years with support from the Maternal and Child Health Bureau of the Health Resources and Services Administration in the Department of Health and Human Services. The NSCH sampled approximately 100,000 children in 2012 and was designed to contain a large enough number of children in each state to enable state-level comparisons of collected information (National Survey of Children's Health, 2012). The survey provides weights to accurately represent the population of noninstitutionalized children ages 0–17 nationally and within each state. We weight the data accordingly in all of the calculations performed with the survey.

The NSCH includes questions regarding whether a child is currently diagnosed with ASD, whether they currently have health insurance, and, if so, the type of health insurance plan. The unweighted sample size for the number of children diagnosed with ASD is 1,624 and weighted estimates from the NSCH survey data indicate a prevalence of ASD of 1.57 percent across U.S. states.[2] The NSCH questions regarding type of health insurance plan only ask specifically about commercial health insurance. Consequently, all individuals who say they have health insurance but say they do not have commercial health insurance we categorize as being in public health insurance (Medicaid). Although this estimate of the number of children with ASD in Medicaid is likely to be an overestimate, we believe this is the best and most current publicly available estimate regarding the number of children in Medicaid diagnosed with ASD. The NSCH does not collect information about ABA utilization rates.

---

[2]   Given the unweighted sample sizes, the state-level ASD populations will be estimated with error. We considered increasing the state sample sizes by adding an earlier year of data. But given the rapid increases in ASD diagnosis rates over time, combined with variation across states in diagnosis rates, we preferred to err on the side of using smaller sample sizes and only using information from the most recent data year available.

Information on ABA Utilization Rates

We searched both the academic and policy literatures for information on state-level ABA utilization rates in the public and commercial health insurance sectors, but we were unable to find any sources with the necessary information on utilization by state and health insurance type. Regarding utilization, the literature consisted primarily of studies investigating the number of hours per week needed to achieve efficacy. To identify state-level utilization rates, we used commercial insurance data from the MarketScan databases, which include a large number of deidentified, individual-level claims for medical services submitted to insurers. To identify children with ASD using ABA services, we used the criteria (ICD-9, CPT, and HCPCS codes) described earlier. Once children with ASD were identified, we used information on the number of days that children were enrolled in a given year and information on the quantities of ABA services consumed to identify the mean annual ABA utilization rates measured in days by state. For external validity, we only used information from states with data for at least ten children. Thus, commercial health plan utilization data was available for 18 states. Mean weekly utilization rates of one-to-one ABA therapy ranged from approximately three units (45 minutes) per week to 34 units (8.5 hours) per week.

As noted, we were not able to identify any information on state-level Medicaid ABA utilization rates. To address this issue, we conducted several sensitivity checks that applied state-level commercial utilization rates for that state's Medicaid population. In the simplest analyses, we applied data on utilization rates from the commercial health insurance system in a particular state to the Medicaid enrollees in the same state. We performed another round of imputations; for states where we have Medicaid reimbursement data but do not have commercial insurance utilization data, we also applied commercial utilization rates to Medicaid enrollees by taking the mean utilization from all of the available state level commercial insurance data.

Mean U.S. Reimbursement Rates: Weighted Mean Calculations

We combined all the available information on state-level commercial and public ABA reimbursement rates, the number of children diagnosed with ASD in commercial and public health insurance plans, and utilization rates to estimate a mean national ABA reimbursement rate.[3] To ensure that we utilized all the available state-level information on ABA reimbursement rates, we performed several calculation methods employing imputations of missing utilization rates for children diagnosed with ASD in the Medicaid system. Twenty-four states used Medicaid waivers to provide these services in 2014; Medicaid reimbursement rates for ABA services were identified for 22 states. (States are listed along with corresponding data in Table 3.4)

We estimated a mean national reimbursement rate using several methods, as depending on the state, data could be missing for commercial insurance reimbursement rates, Medicaid reimbursement rates, or service utilization. The number of states providing data for each calculation method is displayed in Table 3.7. In the simplest calculation, we performed the weighted mean calculations using information on the number of children diagnosed with ASD in the commercial and Medicaid insurance systems and do not use utilization information. This calculation does not incorporate differences in utilization rates across states in calculating mean reimbursement.

We performed this calculation first for states where we have information on reimbursement rates from both the Medicaid and commercial health insurance systems (Calculation 1 in Table 3.7). We also performed this calculation relaxing the restriction that information be available in a given state from both the commercial and Medicaid systems (Calculation 2 in Table 3.7). Hence, if we had only Medicaid or only commercial health insurance reimbursement data for a state, the state was included. There are 38 such states.

We then performed the calculations adding available data on ABA utilization rates. We first include only the states where we have data on both commercial and Medicaid reimbursement rates (Calculation 3 in Table 3.7). In this calculation, we used commercial utilization rates to impute utilization for Medicaid enrollees within that particular state. We then perform a second calculation relaxing the

---

[3]   In this case, *national* means that we use all of the relevant state-level information that we collected.

Table 3.7
Number of States Included in Each Calculation Method for H2019

Calculation	Reimbursement Rates	Utilization Data	States (N)
1	States with rates for both sectors	Not used	13
2	States with rates for at least one sector	Not used	38
3	States with rates for both sectors	Limited to states with commercial utilization rates	9
4	States with rates for at least one sector	Limited to states with commercial utilization rates	18
5	States with rates for both sectors	National utilization rate used for states without rates	13
6	States with rates for at least one sector	National utilization rate used for states without rates	38

restriction that information be available in a given state from both the commercial and Medicaid systems, so again, 18 states were included (Calculation 4 in Table 3.7).

In the final set of calculations, we impute the mean commercial health insurance utilization rate for states with reimbursement rates but no utilization information.[4] Similar to the previous calculations, we perform the weighted mean calculation first for states where we have both commercial and Medicaid reimbursement rates (Calculation 5 in Table 3.7). We then relax this condition and use data from all 38 states where we have a commercial or a Medicaid reimbursement rate (Calculation 6 in Table 3.7).

In this section, we present findings for specific services related to ABA. As mentioned previously, the American Medical Association in 2014 published, for the first time, CPT Category III codes for ABA services (American Medical Association, 2014). We indicate which of these new codes correspond to specific ABA services. However, we did not use these new codes to collect reimbursement data, as few state Medicaid programs had implemented these codes as of our data col-

---

[4] For these imputations, we take a weighted average across all the available states.

lection period, and the latest available commercial insurance data was collected in 2013. Overall, we found that national rates estimated from weighting the reimbursement rates by the number of children diagnosed with ASD in the commercial and public health insurance systems were similar to national rates estimated using additional information on utilization rates. Given that we are not able to estimate utilization rates in the Medicaid system and the similarity of results across different methods, we present national estimated means derived just from weighting with the number of children diagnosed with ASD in a state's public and commercial health insurance systems. The Appendix presents the full set of results for each of the methods described.

One-to-One Therapy by Paraprofessional (suggested new CPT III codes 0364T/0365T)

The weighted mean calculation used commercial insurance reimbursement of H2019 and Medicaid reimbursement for one-on-one ABA provided by those with less than master's degree or unspecified education level. Weighted mean reimbursement rate is $16.29 for 15-minute increments, for an hourly rate of $65.16.

Supervision (suggested new CPT III codes 0360T/0361T), Treatment Plan Update (suggested new CPT III codes 0368T/0369T)

We calculated weighted mean reimbursement rates from commercial health insurance and Medicaid for master's- and doctoral-level providers (H2012, invoiced in hourly increments in commercial insurance data, specific hourly rates for master's- and doctoral-level providers in Medicaid autism waivers). Mean hourly reimbursement rate is $94.72.

Combined ABA Assessment and Treatment Plan Development (suggested new CPT III code 0359T)

We calculated a weighted mean of the sum of reimbursement rates for H0031 and H0032 using only data from the commercial health insurance system, as Medicaid rates specific to ASD could not be identified. The commercial insurance data came from invoices specifically from children with ASD. The mean reimbursement rate for these two services combined was $190.27. However, as these codes may not reflect the time needed for initial Functional Behavioral Assessment and Analysis, the hourly rate used for supervision multiplied by the number of hours involved may be a more accurate estimate of the reimbursement for this service.

Family Guidance (suggested CPT code 0370T)

We were unable to identify sufficient reimbursement rate data to calculate a weighted mean because separate billing for this service is fairly new to ABA providers. This CPT code was implemented in summer 2014.

The above are weighted mean U.S. reimbursement rates; thus, there are many localities where prevailing rates are much higher or lower than the weighted mean. Per Federal Register Notice 80 FR 30664 (DoD, 2015), TRICARE plans to use the Geographic Pricing Cost Index (GPCI), which considers practice costs, malpractice, and cost of living, to develop specific reimbursement rates for each Civilian Health and Medical Program of the Uniformed Services (CHAMPUS) maximum allowable charge (CMAC) locality in the United States. Therefore, we highlight the fact that the weighted average calculations presented in this document use state-level reimbursement rates as they are. Real-world rates implicitly adjust for existing geographic cost differences; i.e., the California rate already accounts for the fact that the cost of practicing in that state is likely to be higher than, for example, the cost of practicing in North Carolina. We also emphasize that the commercial reimbursement rates used in the calculations are based on mean third-party payments to the provider, excluding the patient's out-of-pocket cost. Finally, the calculations were based on 2013 commercial data, as this was the most recent data available.

Summary

We identified information on state Medicaid ABA provider reimbursement rates from 22 states and calculated state-level ABA commercial insurance rates from 29 states. Weighted average calculations using all the available Medicaid and commercial insurance rates resulted in a mean hourly rate for one-to-one ABA by providers without a master's degree or doctorate of $65.16 and a mean hourly rate for BCBA of BCBA-D of $94.72. Cross-state data also suggest some dispersion around these means, as we find a standard deviation of $40 for the unweighted commercial insurance BCBA values and $28 for commercial insurance BCBA values. The proposed TRICARE rate of $68 for BCBAs is substantially below the weighted mean reimbursement rate of commercial and public insurers. Due to the identified means and dispersion, one national TRICARE rate for ABA providers will lead to substantial misalignment across states between TRICARE rates and rates from other insurers, particularly for BCBAs.

CHAPTER FOUR

Potential Provider Shortage Areas

To identify locations of potential ABA provider shortages, we obtained data from the BACB on the location of all certified ABA providers in the United States and then calculated the number of children with ASD in TRICARE per each provider in locations throughout the United States.

In order to assist in our analysis, TRICARE provided the number of potential ABA service users by U.S. Postal Service ZIP code at the three-digit level. TRICARE beneficiaries ages 0 to 18 (inclusive) with ASD receiving services from 2012 to 2014 were identified from the nine ICD-9 ASD diagnosis codes appearing on either direct care records or purchased care claims. Three-digit ZIP codes (instead of five-digit ZIP codes) were used to reduce the chances of having small cell sizes with ten or fewer beneficiaries, as health data systems routinely suppress information on cell sizes with fewer than 11 beneficiaries in a specific geographic area to ensure protection of personal health identification information. Of 860 three-digit ZIP code areas, however, only 520 had 11 or more users; the rest still had fewer than 11 beneficiaries with ASD. To solve this problem, each three-digit ZIP code location with one or more ABA users was assigned to a group ("combined ZIP code location") based on contiguous geographic area. This resulted in a total of 565 "combined ZIP code locations" (or 45 more ZIP code locations than if they had only retained the 520 three-digit ZIP codes with 11 or more users). Of these 565 "combined ZIP code locations," 394 (or 70 percent) contain only one three-digit ZIP code area, 108 (or 19 percent) contain two combined three-digit ZIP code areas,

29 (5 percent) contain three combined three-digit ZIP code areas, and 34 (or 6 percent) contain four or more three-digit ZIP code areas.

Locations for all master's- and doctoral-level Behavioral Analysts and Assistant Behavior Analysts as of May 2015 were obtained from the BACB. The data on location of these providers were merged with the data on locations of potential ABA users (children with ASD diagnoses) in TRICARE and a ratio of the number of board certified providers to potential users was calculated for each "combined ZIP code location" described above. Ratios were calculated separately for master's-level Behavior Analysts, doctoral-level Behavioral Analysts, Assistant Behavior Analysts, and total board certified providers. Our analysis included only children with ASD in TRICARE. Of course, a more accurate way to identify locations of potential provider shortages would be to include the entire number of children with ASD in each three-digit ZIP code location. Unfortunately, such data is not available by ZIP code.

Locations with No Board Certified ABA Providers

We identified 15 locations with children with ASD in TRICARE (potential ABA users) but no board certified providers as of January 2015. The locations with potential TRICARE ABA users but no board certified ABA providers are shaded in green in Figures 4.1 and 4.2. Figure 4.1 also displays nearby military installations, and Figure 4.2 displays major cities. The number of TRICARE beneficiaries with ASD living in the locations with no board certified providers ranges from 12 in southern Missouri to 288 in western Idaho; the number in each location is superimposed in bold.

We provided the project sponsor with an Excel file containing the number of children with ASD in TRICARE per each type of board certified ABA provider, and total board certified providers, in each "combined ZIP code location." Locations with a high number of potential TRICARE ABA users per certified provider include several locations in the Southwest (San Diego, southern Arizona, and west Texas) and in the Southeast (Virginia, South Carolina, Georgia, and

Figure 4.1
Map with Locations with Potential TRICARE ABA Users but No Board
Certified ABA Providers, with Military Installations

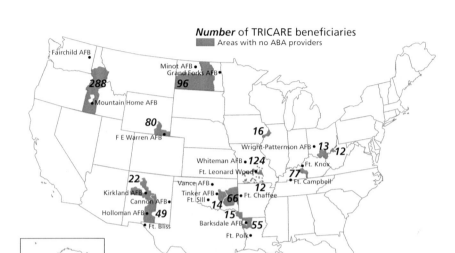

Note: Number of potential ABA users in TRICARE, birth–18 years with ASD,
in combined ZIP code locations with no ABA providers.

RAND RR1334-4.1

Alabama). These locations have more than 100 potential TRICARE
users for each BCBA.

There are currently no best practice standards as to the number
of certified providers per number of children with ASD. The American
Academy of Pediatrics recommends at least 25 hours per week of early
intervention for young children with ASD (Myers and Johnson, 2007).
However, this is not specific to ABA therapy. According to 2012 BACB
guidelines, the average caseload for a Behavior Analyst supervising
focused treatment without support from an Assistant Behavior Analyst
is ten to 15 children; with a supporting Assistant Behavior Analyst, the
average caseload is 16 to 24 children (BACB, 2012).

Our analysis included only children with ASD in TRICARE. A more
accurate way to identify locations of potential provider shortages would be
to include the entire number of children with ASD in each three-digit ZIP
code location. Unfortunately, such data is not available by ZIP code.

Figure 4.2
**Map with Locations with Potential TRICARE ABA Users but No Board
Certified ABA Providers with Major Cities Displayed**

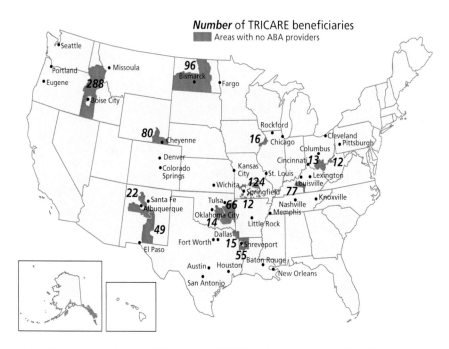

Note: Number of potential ABA users in TRICARE, birth–18 years with ASD,
in combined ZIP code locations with no ABA providers.

RAND RR1334-4.2

CHAPTER FIVE

Discussion

Conclusions

The treatment of ASD is a rapidly developing field with several early intervention options. ABA is widely accepted, however, the insurance coverage, reimbursement rates, and CPT coding for ASD treatments (including ABA) are still evolving. In some instances, insurance coverage has changed as a result of legislation, new evidence of effectiveness, and court decisions.

TRICARE's ABA coverage also is evolving in response to scientific evidence; changes in health insurance coverage for ABA; and feedback from beneficiaries, ABA providers, and ASD experts. The TRICARE ACD helps to address beneficiary concerns by combining all ABA services into one demonstration project and expands coverage for ABA to all beneficiaries with ASD, removes the annual cap on reimbursement, and aligns copays with other TRICARE copays.

Coverage and reimbursement rates for ABA vary widely in both commercial plans and Medicaid. We were asked to compare TRICARE's proposed rate of $68 per hour for one-to-one ABA therapy provided by a BCBA or BCBA-D, reduced from $125 per hour, with the current U.S. market. The proposed $68-per-hour rate is below the mean commercial insurance rate in ten of the 17 states, where data was available, and above the mean commercial insurance rate in the other seven states. Similarly, compared with 14 states that specify rates for master's- and doctoral-level ABA providers in Medicaid, the $68-per-hour rate is below the reimbursement rate in 11 states.

We estimated mean U.S. reimbursement rates for ABA services based on local Medicaid and commercial insurance reimbursement rates, weighted by the number of children with ASD covered by each type of insurance in each location. The weighted mean U.S. reimbursement rate for one-to-one therapy by paraprofessionals was $65.16 per hour. This calculation used commercial insurance reimbursement of H2019 and Medicaid reimbursement for one-to-one ABA provided by those with less than a master's degree or unspecified education level. It is possible that some invoices for BCBAs were included in the rate calculations where education level was unspecified. The estimated weighted mean U.S. reimbursement rate for treatment provided by master's- or doctoral-level providers (BCBA, CPT code H2012) is $94.72.

The development of new reimbursement rates must recognize that our analyses used commercial insurance data from 2013 and Medicaid reimbursement rate data from 2014 and adjust accordingly. In addition, we identified geographic regions where there is a potential need for ABA services for TRICARE beneficiaries with ASD but no or very few board certified ABA providers.

Policy Implications

We identified reimbursement rates that varied widely throughout the United States. TRICARE proposes to develop reimbursement rates by applying the GPCI to weighted mean national reimbursement rates for ABA. This project analyzed commercial insurance data from 2013, the most recent full year of data available. With few exceptions (see Table 3.1 in Chapter Three), Medicaid rates were current as of January 2015. Results from this study indicate that the proposed rate of $68 for BCBA is not consistent with reimbursement rates from the commercial and public insurers; if adopted, these rates might lead providers either to leave TRICARE's networks or to prioritize ASD children from other health insurers over TRICARE-covered children.

TRICARE's ACD, which is scheduled to end on December 31, 2018, presents a unique opportunity to evaluate a benefit in the context of a rapidly evolving field. TRICARE will need to re-evaluate reimbursement rates before the ACD ends in order to calculate an updated national reimbursement rate based on the most recent data. TRICARE should evaluate ABA utilization regularly and continuously monitor the adequacy of the ABA provider network. During the course of the ACD, there likely will be numerous changes in commercial and public health insurance coverage for ASD treatments, including ABA, due to evolving policies and legislation. TRICARE should remain engaged in these discussions about changes in ABA coverage in other private and public health insurance plans. The uptake of CPT Category III codes for ABA also will make it easier to evaluate utilization patterns of and reimbursement rates for ABA services.

Sensitivity Analysis Results

This appendix contains the results from each sensitivity analysis performed in calculating weighted mean U.S. reimbursement rates. We describe the different scenarios in greater detail on pp. 38–39 of the report. Each of the following tables contain information on whether reimbursement rate data were only taken from states where information was available from both the public and private sectors, whether utilization information was used in the calculation, the number of unique states that entered into the calculation, and the resulting reimbursement rate.

Table A.1
H2019 Therapeutic Behavioral Services, per Hour

Calculation	Reimbursement Rates	Utilization Data	Mean	States (N)
1	States with rates for both sectors	Not used	$63.60	13
2	States with rates for at least one sector	Not used	$65.16	38
3	States with rates for both sectors	Limited to states with commercial utilization rates	$59.20	9
4	States with rates for at least one sector	Limited to states with commercial utilization rates	$63.24	18
5	States with rates for both sectors	National utilization rate used for states without rates	$59.20	13
6	States with rates for at least one sector	National utilization rate used for states without rates	$62.84	38

Table A.2
Behavioral Health per Hour–H2012 in Commercial Insurance or Master's- or Doctoral-Level ABA provider in Medicaid

Calculation	Reimbursement Rates	Utilization Data	Mean	States (N)
1	States with rates for both sectors	Not used	$88.64	8
2	States with rates for at least one sector	Not used	$94.72	23
3	States with rates for both sectors	Limited to states with commercial utilization rates	$93.72	1
4	States with rates for at least one sector	Limited to states with commercial utilization rates	$92.64	12
5	States with rates for both sectors	National utilization rate used for states without rates	$84.24	8
6	States with rates for at least one sector	National utilization rate used for states without rates	$94.24	23

Abbreviations

ABA	Applied Behavior Analysis
ACD	Autism Care Demonstration
ADFM	active-duty family member
ADOS-2	Autism Diagnosis Observations Scale, Second Edition
ASD	autism spectrum disorder
BACB	Behavior Analyst Certification Board
BCBA	Board Certified Behavior Analyst
BCBA-D	Board Certified Behavior Analyst–Doctoral
BCaBA	Board Certified Assistant Behavior Analyst
CDC	Centers for Disease Control and Prevention
CFR	Code of Federal Regulations
CHAMPUS	Civilian Health and Medical Program of the Uniformed Services
CMAC	CHAMPUS Maximum Allowable Charge
CMS	Centers for Medicare and Medicaid Services
CPT	Current Procedural Terminology
DHA	Defense Health Agency

DoD	Department of Defense
ECHO	Extended Care Health Option
EFMP	Exceptional Family Member Program
FR	Federal Register
FY	fiscal year
GPCI	Geographic Practice Cost Index
HCPCS	Healthcare Common Procedure Coding System
IBI	Intensive Behavioral Intervention
ICD-9	International Classification of Diseases, Ninth Revision
MCSC	Managed Care Support Contractor
NADFM	non-active-duty family member
NDAA	National Defense Authorization Act
NDRI	National Defense Research Institute
NR	not reported
NSCH	National Survey of Children's Health
OUSD [P&R]	Office of the Undersecretary of Defense for Personnel and Readiness
PDD-NOS	pervasive developmental disorder or not otherwise specified
P-PCM	physician-primary care manager
PFPWD	Program for Persons with Disabilities
RBT	registered behavior technician
TRO	TRICARE regional office

References

American Medical Association, *CPT Assistant: Official Source for CPT Coding Guidance*, Vol. 24, No. 6, 2014.

American Psychiatric Association, *Diagnostic and Statistical Manual of Mental Disorders (DSM-5)*, Fifth Edition, Washington, D.C., 2013.

Anthem Blue Cross Blue Shield, "Adaptive Behavioral Treatment for Autism Spectrum Disorder. Guideline # CG-BEH-02," 2015. As of October 12, 2015:
https://www.anthem.com/medicalpolicies/guidelines/gl_pw_c166121.htm

BACB—*See* Behavior Analyst Certification Board.

Behavior Analyst Certification Board, *Guidelines: Health Plan Coverage of Applied Behavior Analysis Treatment for Autism Spectrum Disorder*, Tallahassee, Fla., 2012.

———, "About the BACB," 2015. As of August 11, 2015:
http://bacb.com/about-the-bacb/

CDC—*See* Centers for Disease Control and Prevention.

Centers for Disease Control and Prevention, "Autism Spectrum Disorder (ASD): Treatments," February 24, 2015. As of July 16, 2015:
http://www.cdc.gov/ncbddd/autism/treatment.html

DHA—*See* Defense Health Agency.

Defense Health Agency, "Autism Care Demonstration," 2015a. As of July 16, 2015:
http://www.tricare.mil/autism

———, "TRICARE Operations Manual, TOM 6010.56-M," 2015b. As of December 23, 2015:
http://manuals.tricare.osd.mil/DisplayManual.aspx?SeriesId=OPERATIONS

DoD—*See* U.S. Department of Defense.

Lord, Catherine, Michael Rutter, Pamela C. DiLavore, Susan Risi, Katherine Gotham, and Somer L. Bishop, *Autism Diagnostic Observation Schedule™, Second Edition (ADOS™-2)*, second edition, Torrance, Calif.: Western Psychological Services, 2012. As of December 23, 2015: http://www.wpspublish.com/store/p/2648/ autism-diagnostic-observation-schedule-second-edition-ados-2

Maglione, Margaret. A., Daphna Gans, Lopamudra Das, Justin Timbie, and Connie Kasari, "Nonmedical Interventions for Children with ASD: Recommended Guidelines and Further Research Needs," *Pediatrics*, Vol. 130 Supp. 2, 2012, pp. S169–178. As of December 16, 2015: http://www.ncbi.nlm.nih.gov/pubmed/23118248

Mann, Cindy, *Clarification of Medicaid Coverage of Services to Children with Autism*, Baltimore, Md.: Centers for Medicare or Medicaid Services, Department of Health and Human Services, 2014.

Myers, Scott. M., and Chris P. Johnson, "Management of Children with Autism Spectrum Disorders," *Pediatrics*, Vol. 120, No. 5, November 2007, pp. 1162-1182. As of December 23, 2015: http://www.ncbi.nlm.nih.gov/pubmed/17967921

National Conference of State Legislatures, "Insurance Coverage for Autism," 2012. As of October 16, 2015: http://www.ncsl.org/research/health/autism-and-insurance-coverage-state-laws. aspx

National Survey of Children's Health, homepage, 2012. As of December 16, 2015: http://childhealthdata.org/learn/NSCH

Office of the Secretary of Defense, *32 CFR § 199.2*, Washington, D.C., 2011.

———, *32 CFR § 199.5*, Washington, D.C., 2004.

———, *32 CFR § 199.4(g)(1)*, 2010.

Priority Health, *Autism Spectrum & Pervasive Developmental Disorders*, Medical Policy No. 91579-R3, 2014.

Public Law 107-107, National Defense Authorization Act for Fiscal Year 2002, 2015. As of December 21, 2015: http://thomas.loc.gov/cgi-bin/query/z?c107:S.1438.ENR:

Public Law 109-364, John Warner National Defense Authorization Act for Fiscal Year 2007, 2006. As of December 21, 2015: http://thomas.loc.gov/cgi-bin/bdquery/z?d109:h.r.05122:

Public Law 112-479, National Defense Authorization Act for Fiscal Year 2013, 2012. As of December 23, 2015: https://www.gpo.gov/fdsys/pkg/PLAW-112publ239/content-detail.html

Selden, T. M., G. M. Kenney, M. S. Pantell, and J. Ruhter, "Cost Sharing in Medicaid and CHIP: How does it Affect Out-of-Pocket Spending?" *Health Affairs,* Vol. 28, No. 4, 2009, pp. w607–619. As of December 22, 2015: http://www.ncbi.nlm.nih.gov/pubmed/19491137

Sparrow, Sara S., Domenic V. Cicchetti, and David A. Balla, *Vineland Adaptive Behavior Scales,* 2nd ed., Circle Pines, Minn.: American Guidance Service, 2005.

TRICARE Policy Manual 6010.57-M, February 1, 2008. As of December 23, 2015: http://manuals.tricare.osd.mil

Tufts Health Plan, *Medical Necessity Guidelines: ABA (Applied Behavioral Analysis) Therapy for Autism Spectrum Disorders: Rhode Island Products,* 2014.

United Health Care, *Intensive Behavioral Therapy for Autism Spectrum Disorders,* United HealthCare Services, Inc., Medical Policy, 2014.

U.S. Department of Defense, "TRICARE: Individual Case Management Program; Program for Persons With Disabilities; Extended Benefits for Disabled Family Members of Active Duty Service Members; Custodial Care," *Federal Register* 32, No. 199, July 28,2004. As of December 21, 2015: https://federalregister.gov/a/04-16932

———, Notice, "Autism Services Demonstration Project for TRICARE Beneficiaries under the Extended Health Care Option Program," *Federal Register* 72, No. 68130, December 4, 2007.

———, Notice, "Autism Services Demonstration Project for TRICARE Beneficiaries Under the Extended Health Care Option," *Federal Register* 75, No. 8927, February 26, 2010. As of December 22, 2015: https://federalregister.gov/a/2010-3990

———, Notice, "Extension of Autism Services Demonstration Project for TRICARE Beneficiaries Under the Extended Care Health Option," *Federal Register* 76, No. 80903, December 27, 2011. As of December 22, 2015: https://federalregister.gov/a/2011-33064

———, Notice, "Comprehensive Autism Care Demonstration," *Federal Register* 79, No. 34291, June 16, 2014. As of December 22, 2015: https://federalregister.gov/a/2014-14023

———, Amendment, "Comprehensive Autism Care Demonstration Amendment," *Federal Register* 80, No. 30664, May 29, 2015. As of December 22, 2015: https://federalregister.gov/a/2015-13001

Zickafoose, Joe, Kate Stewart, Lauren Hula, Rebecca Coughlin, and Michelle Kloc, Mathematica Policy Research, "Children with Autism and Developmental Disabilities in the Military Health System: Prevalence and Demographic and Military-Related Characteristics," memorandum to Tom Williams, November 7, 2013.